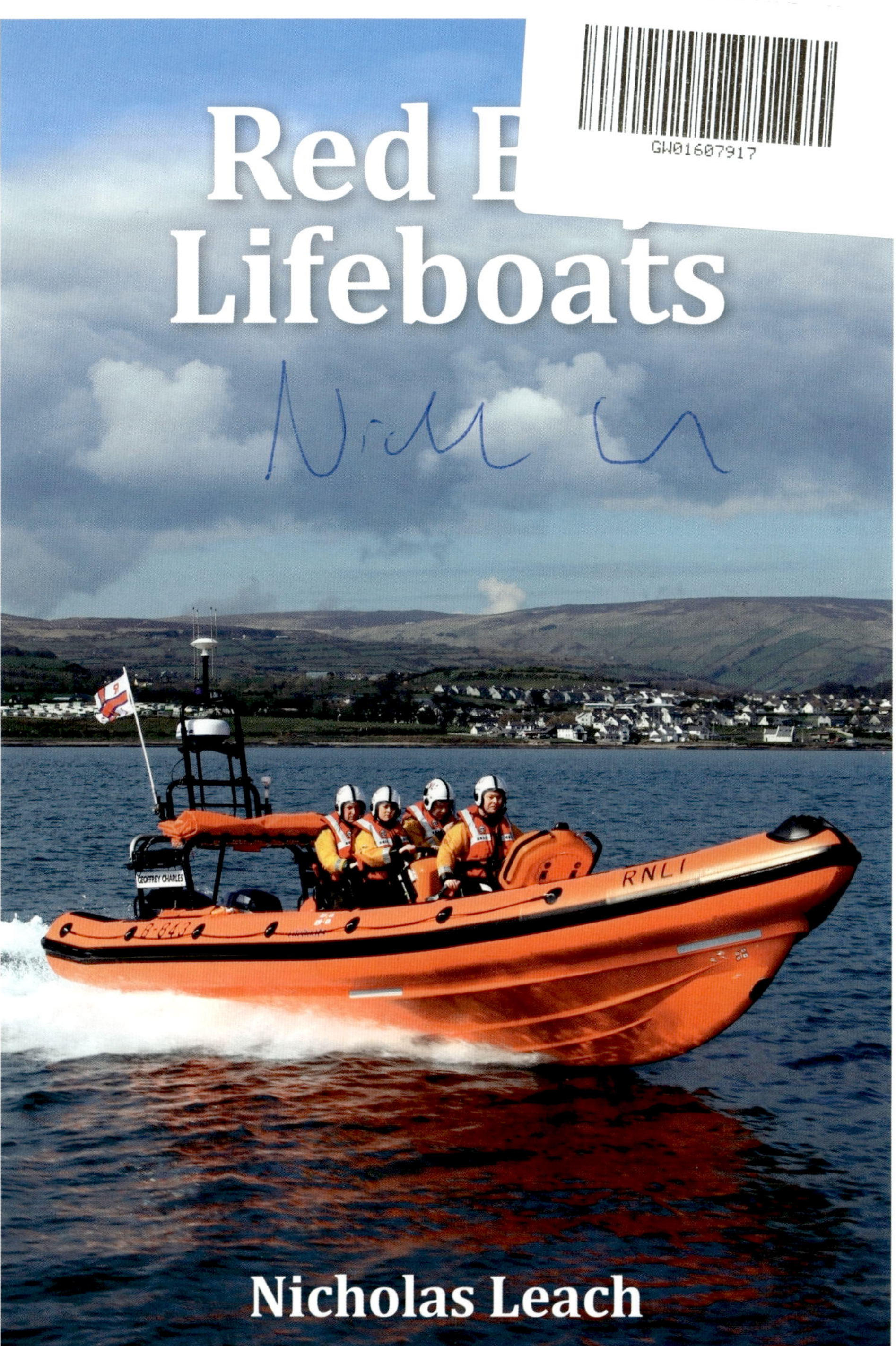
Red B
Lifeboats
GEOFFREY CHARLES
RNLI
Nicholas Leach

Red Bay lifeboat crew March 2011

On the boat, from left to right, are Sean Harvey, Emmet Connon, Darren McGinley, Gary McAlister and James Sharpe. Standing to the left of the boat, from left to right, back to front: Paddy McLaughlin, John Walsh, Paddy O'Hagan, Donal McAlister, Dr Dermot Grant, Danny Bevan, Rita O'Neill, Joe Burns, Charles Stewart, Dr Louise McIlwaine and Kevin Allen. Standing to the right of the boat, from left to right, back to front: Sammy Goligher, Gary Fyfe, Padraig Mitchell, Donal Black, Andrew McAlister, Stephen Conway, Dan McCollam, Neil Workman, Gerry O'Neill, Kevin McDonnell and Alan Murphy (Lifeboat Operations Manager)

Contents

ISBN 9780956456045

Published by Foxglove Publishing Ltd
Foxglove House, Shute Hill, Lichfield, Staffs WS13 8DB
t > 01543 673594
e > foxglove.media@btinternet.com

Acknowledgements • This book could not have been written without the help and support of the Red Bay lifeboat crew, particularly Paddy McLaughlin, who answered many questions, found much of the information and photos for inclusion and was the driving force behind the project's success. Stephen Conway and various other crew members also provided help and information. At RNLI Headquarters in Poole, thanks to Brian Wead and his staff at the Service Information Section, Nathan Williams and Eleanor Driscoll for supplying images, and Liz Cook, Editorial Manager.

Layout and design by Nicholas Leach
Printed by W&G Baird, Northern Ireland, through their kind charitable donation

Introduction

The Red Bay lifeboat station was established in 1972 at Cushendall, a small village at the mouth of the river Dall on the Antrim Coast road between Larne and Ballycastle. The neighbouring lifeboat stations are at Portrush to the north and Larne to the south, but as the latter was not established until 1994, for many years the offshore lifeboats at Portrush and Donaghadee, at the mouth of Belfast Lough, were the only ones in the area. Portrush lifeboat station was opened in 1860, Donaghadee in 1910 taking over from the station at nearby Groomsport founded in 1858 and a station at Carrickfergus, in Belfast Lough, was operated between 1896 and 1913. Across the Irish Sea in Scotland, Campbeltown lifeboat station, opened in 1861, is one of the closest to Red Bay. A motor lifeboat has operated from there since 1912, and a 17m Severn class lifeboat since 1999.

Although no lifeboat station was operated on the Antrim coast between Portrush and Belfast until 1972, in the nineteenth century a number of medals were awarded by the RNLI for outstanding rescues undertaken by shore boats. On 10 May 1840, when the sloop Industry, of Belfast, was wrecked in bad weather in Glenarm Bay, Lieutenant Lyons, RN, of HM Coastguard Glenarm, with three coastguardsmen and three other men, went off in a

▼ An aerial view of the modern Red Bay lifeboat station in the small village of Cushendall on the coast of County Antrim.

boat and saved her master and the three man crew. For this shore boat rescue, Lieutenant Lyons was awarded the RNLI's Silver medal.

Two other medal-winning rescues were undertaken in the area during the 1850s. On 16 January 1851 the Coleraine schooner Martin parted her anchors at 3pm and drove onto rocks off Rock Point, near Cushendun, in a very heavy gale. With the schooner's boat broken to pieces by the seas passing over her, the master and four crewmen took to a mast. Lieutenant Arthur Kennedy, of HM Coastguard Cushendun, and his crew, unable to launch their boat, carried a country boat over the rocks until they were opposite the wreck, and then launched to help the casualty. They were forced to put back twice because of the very high seas breaking on the shore, but at the third attempt rescued the schooner's crew. For his leadership, Lieutenant Kennedy was awarded the Silver medal by the RNLI.

▲ The memorial plaque to the nine crewmen lost in the steamer Peridot in November 1905 can be seen at Carnlough harbour. (Nicholas Leach)

The other medal-winning service was undertaken on 11 March 1857 after a local farmer tripped over a mooring chain and fell into the sea at Cushendall. John Aiken, a commissioned boatman of HM Coastguard, immediately went into the water after the farmer and, grabbing a mooring chain, swam over to where the man had sunk. When the farmer came to the surface, the coastguardman grabbed him with one hand and supported him for at least five minutes by holding onto the chain with the other hand. He sustained a dislocated arm and severely damaged hand, but saved the man's life, an act for which he too was awarded the Silver medal by the RNLI.

Other wrecks have occurred in the area, including one tragedy on 26 November 1905 when the 200-ton steamship Peridot, built in 1890 and carrying a cargo of coal, was caught out in gale force conditions. En route from Scotland to Carnlough, she was forced to run for the safety of Larne Lough but foundered on Skernaghan Point at Browns Bay and her entire crew of nine were lost. The vessel broke in two and was just visible above the waves, off Skernaghan Point, for a few hours.

The D class inflatables

The RNLI officially established a lifeboat station at Red Bay on 26 August 1972 after a successful period of trials with a D class inflatable inshore lifeboat (ILB). Since May 1972, under the guidance of the Inspector of Irish Lifeboats, Cmdr Brian Miles, late Director of the Institution, and Captain T. L. Scollay, who went on to become the first Honorary Secretary, seventeen local volunteers were trained to use the single-engined inflatable rescue craft. The crew included the one of first female lifeboat members in the RNLI, Joan Murphy. The first services undertaken came on 23 July and 2 August 1972, but the former proved to be a false alarm and on the latter occasion she was not needed, with a yacht caught out in bad weather being helped by others.

The D class inflatable, a type which had been in service with the RNLI for almost a decade by the time Red Bay lifeboat station was established, was the smallest lifeboat in the RNLI fleet having been introduced in 1963. The 16ft inflatable lifeboats, made from tough nylon coated with hypalon, were crewed by between two and four volunteers, powered by a 40hp outboard engine, and able to be launched quickly and easily. They were equipped with VHF radio, flexible fuel tanks, flares, an anchor, a spare propeller, a compass, first aid kit and knife. The ILB's advantage over the conventional lifeboat was its speed which, at twenty knots, was considerably faster than any lifeboat in service during the 1960s. The ILB also has the advantage of being able to go alongside other craft easily, or pick up persons in the water, without causing or suffering damage.

The ILB was initially housed in a small shed at Cushendall, a few hundred metres away from the present site. Funds for the shed's construction were

▶ The scene at Cushendall on 26 August 1972 during the inauguration ceremony of the lifeboat station, with crew members standing by D-196. (All photos by courtesy of Red Bay RNLI unless stated)

ROYAL NATIONAL LIFE-BOAT INSTITUTION
NORTHERN IRELAND

The Chairman and Committee of the Red Bay Branch request the honour of your company at the Inauguration of the

RED BAY INSHORE LIFE-BOAT

at

MEETSON'S SLIPWAY, CUSHENDALL

on SATURDAY, 26th AUGUST, 1972 at 4.00 p.m.

Under the patronage and in the presence of His Excellency The Governor of Northern Ireland and Lady Grey of Naunton

The Life-boat will be blessed after a short service to be conducted jointly by:

REVEREND S. McKEOWN, P.P. REVEREND J. HEATLEY
REVEREND J. LUKE

Guests should arrive by 3.30 p.m.

Please reply on the enclosed postcard

PLEASE BRING THIS CARD WITH YOU – IT IS YOUR ENTRANCE TICKET

◀ Invitation to the inauguration ceremony of Red Bay lifeboat in August 1972.

collected locally, but when Moyle District Council acknowledged the importance of the lifeboat service to the community, a new station was built with much improved slipway facilities. The station was originally designated as being operational during the summer only, which meant that the ILB was available for service between March and October. The crew trained regularly each week, improving their skills in seamanship, boat handling, radio procedure, liaising with Coastguard and exercising with helicopters. In the winter months, when the boat was off station, crew training involved working on improving first-aid techniques and navigation skills and knowledge.

The first and, it turned out, only D class inflatable to serve the station, D-196, was operational for a remarkable fifteen years, giving outstanding service, and gaining a fine record of eighty-four launches on service. She was credited with rescuing forty-seven lives and was involved in the recovery of many valuable small vessels. It is unusual for an ILB to serve for more than ten years, so D-196 was a remarkable craft in many ways. She was taken away for refit only once, in 1984, when the relief ILB D 185, was sent to the station for a short stint.

▶ The lifeboat crew with the D class inflatable in 1988 with, left to right, Tom McLaughlin, Paddy McLaughlin, Donal McAlister, Chris McCarthy, Neil Workman (Honorary Secretary, at front), Andrew McAlister andLiam McCollam.

1972 – 1987

The station, with D-196 as its centrepiece, was officially inaugurated at Metson's Slipway, Cushendall, at 4pm on 26 August 1972, with the Governor of Northern Ireland and Lady Grey of Naunton in attendance. Vice Admiral Sir Arthur Hezlet, KBE, DSO, Northern Irish member of the RNLI's Committee of Management, and Lady Hezlet, formally delivered the ILB to the care of the local branch. T. G. McLaughlin was in the chair for the proceedings and Captain T. Scollay accepted the boat on behalf of the branch. After the inaugural speeches, a short service of dedication was held, during which the lifeboat was blessed by the Very Rev S. McKeown and the Rev J. Heatley.

After the initial two rescues had been performed, but for which the ILB was not needed, the first effective service undertaken by the Red Bay lifeboat came on 14 September 1972, just a fortnight after the official inauguration. D-196 launched to a small motor boat with engine failure four miles off the station, bringing the casualty and her crew of four to safety. D-196 was out again on 15 October 1972, launching to a small motor boat which had capsized, saving the boat and her two crew.

Only two services were performed in 1973, on 1 and 2 September, when D-196 launched to help capsized sailing dinghies on both occasions. No effective services were completed in 1974 and only one was performed in 1975, when D-196 escorted a motor boat with engine failure on 13 June. Almost exactly a year later, on 12 June 1976, the ILB undertook a very efficient and quick rescue after crew member Norris Murray had spotted,

▼ D class inflatable D-196 on exercise.

Getting a station established

“Red Bay lifeboat is based in the village of Cushendall in the Glens of Antrim. It is unusual to name a lifeboat after an area rather than the village or town in which it was based. However the group of local people who initiated the stationing of a lifeboat in the area saw it as not simply a service to Cushendall but to the overall Glens area. Thus the name Red Bay was chosen as it could be identified by the various coastal communities.

There was an obvious need for a lifeboat in the area where the beaches, rocky coastline, towering cliffs and indeed the only inhabited offshore island in Northern Ireland, Rathlin, can be a dangerous place. In 1972 the nearest lifeboats were Portrush, over thirty-two miles by sea, and Donaghadee, thirty-seven miles to the south. In fact, as the crow flies, the nearest lifeboat is Campbeltown, twenty-two miles away, but further round the Mull of Kintyre. An increase in pleasure boating in the area was also a factor, especially after the Cushendall Sailing and Boating Club had been set up in 1962.

A group of locals and visitors identified a need for a rescue service and local families with a maritime or fishing tradition also came together to get the station established. The same people, who ten years earlier had set up Cushendall sailing and Boat Club, began working towards getting a lifeboat station founded. Two incidents highlighted the need for a lifeboat station to be set up, and they involved people getting into difficulty at sea, which could have turned out badly except for local initiative.

The first incident was in 1964 when Vincent Hanna, the Belfast born television journalist, went out in the family rowing boat in the late evening with a student friend. When he lost an oar, the boat drifted out into the Bay where conditions were worse. Mannix McAlister, on returning from checking his salmon nets, discovered his car and trailer at the slipway and was immediately concerned. Assisted by John Finlay, an experienced commercial fisherman, Mannix launched his 18ft salmon boat knowing, with the force six westerly increasing, the casualty could be drifting towards the infamous Garron point. Darkness had fallen when Mannix saw the boat in the large waves formed off Garron. A tow rope was thrown across and, after a slow tow the boats reached the safety of the slipway after midnight.

The second incident, a few years later, involved two capsized sailing dinghies, north of Red Bay. After repeated attempts to right the craft, the occupants became exhausted and gave up, drifting in strong ebb tide towards Cushendun before Mannix McAlister became aware of their plight and went to their aid in his open salmon boat. The survivors were landed, suffering from hypothermia, and had to receive urgent attention in McAlister’s home.

The initial committee was made up of a mix of local people with a professional or recreational interest in the sea. The chairman was businessman and experienced leisure boatman Tom McLaughlin, the first Honorary Secretary a former Sea captain, Tommy Scollay, and the Branch chair was Mrs Blaney, wife of a sea captain. Other committee members included Mannix McAlister and various other boat club members.

The first crew were Liam McCollam, Oliver McCollam, Robert McCollam, Terence McCollam, Joan Murphy, Donal McAlister, Norris Murray, Dan McCollam, Oliver McMullan, Patrick McCollam, Hugh Ward, David Murphy, Pat McCollam, Con Emerson, Bob Gilliland, Charlie Metson, and Bobby Wheeler, as well as Joan Murphy, one of the first women lifeboat crew members in the RNLI.

The lifeboat was delivered by the Irish inspector Brian Miles in June 1972 for initial trials. It actually had its first incident before reaching Red Bay. Cmdr Brian Miles had an ‘altercation’ with the Black Arch on the Antrim coast road and the boat needed to be patched and the trailer repaired before trials could begin - an inauspicious start, but no deterrent to the enthusiastic crew. Indeed as one of crew stated at the time, ‘the only thing that was deflated by the incident was Brian Miles and the boat!’”

Andrew McAlister

from his home, a sailing dinghy in trouble. He informed the deputy launching authority and the crew was immediately called out.

The ILB launched at 7.18pm and set course for the dinghy, which was two miles south-east of the station. The wind was westerly, strong force six gusting to near gale force seven, making conditions very difficult for the inshore lifeboat. However, the casualty was quickly reached and the dinghy, with a three man crew, was found to have her mast broken in three places. She was therefore towed back to the slipway and her crew were safely brought ashore. The service had taken just half an hour, and the ILB was rehoused and ready for service again at 7.50pm.

During the late 1970s the ILB was undertaking three or four services a year, mostly to sailing dinghies and motor boats that had got into difficulty, and this pattern continued into the 1980s, with one service in 1981 proving to be a particularly fine one. On the evening of 29 June 1981 John McAllister was working at Garron Point, east of the lifeboat station, when he saw people in a small dinghy, waving for help. He immediately telephoned the deputy launching authority at 7.05pm and five minutes later D-196 was launched, manned by helmsman Donal McAlister and crew member Tom McLaughlin. A gentle to moderate breeze was blowing from the north-west, and the sea was choppy.

On reaching the search area, no sign could be found of the casualty, so the lifeboat rendezvoused with McAllister at Garron Point. He told the crew where the dinghy had been when he last saw her, and so the ILB continued her search of the area he indicated. At 7.40pm the dinghy, an 8ft boat with

▼ D-196 on the launching trolley, which was manhandled into the water to get the boat afloat.

◀ D-196 on her launching trolley outside the ILB house with the crew and local coastguards.

a small outboard engine, was spotted three miles north-east of Glenarm Head. The lifeboat was soon alongside the casualty, three children and a man were transferred onto the lifeboat, and the dinghy was towed back to the station slipway. By 8.30pm the lifeboat had been rehoused and was ready for service. For his help with this service, a letter of appreciation signed by Rear Admiral W. J. Graham, the RNLI Director, was sent to John McAllister.

On 1 August 1982 the lifeboat was called into action during the Cushendall Regatta, the seventeenth annual event organised by the local Sailing and Boating Club. The lifeboat crew had performed a simulated rescue for the benefit of the crowds during the fund-raising day, but were then called out for real after a 13ft fibreglass dinghy was swamped by a heavy swell and started drifting, full of water. Crew members, and brothers, John and Patrick McLaughlin, returned to the ILB house and launched D-196 within minutes of the alarm. As the casualty was overloaded, the ILB stood by until a fishing

▼ The small ILB house built at Cushendall in 1973, funded by Moyle District Council. The house was used until 1995.

1972 – 1987

▶ D class inflatable D-196 heading out from Red Bay on exercise in 1972.

boat had reached it and was able to take off some of those on board. The ILB saved the eight people on board the dinghy, with the help of fisherman Eamon Darragh, and then towed the small dory back to shore.

On 28 June 1985 D-196 was launched on service after a boat with nine children on board got into difficulties with the engine failing. The ILB was launched late at night after reports that the children were in trouble close inshore at the south end of the bay. The 24ft cabin cruiser Maggie Jane was found by the lifeboat crew, with nine children and two adults on board, suffering engine failure. Once on scene, the ILB crew immediately took the eleven people off the cruiser and landed them ashore, before towing the casualty to safety.

▼ D class inflatable D-196 returning to station.

Although the D class ILB had proved her worth on many rescues in Red Bay, by the mid-1980s the local branch officials and crew believed that a larger lifeboat was needed. They had always felt somewhat uneasy about the use of a single-engined inflatable lifeboat working along the remote and rugged shores of the North Antrim coast, and so approached the RNLI, asking the Institution to consider placing a more capable lifeboat at the station. At the same time, the need for the lifeboat to be on service in the area all year round had also become pressing.

As a result, a series of trials were undertaken during 1985 and 1986 with the larger, heavier twin-engined C class inflatable and in July 1985 the 17ft 6in Zodiac Mk.IV type inflatable, number C-510, came to the station as part of the evaluation trials. She performed two services during her short stay at Cushendall, helping a capsized canoe on 11 July and bringing in a broken down power boat three days later.

Following the success of the trials with the C class inflatable, in August 1986 D-196, having given outstanding service, was replaced by one and left the station for the last time. During 1986, her last year of service, she had been kept busy, completing nine effective services in the space of four months between April and August. On 6 April 1985, in force five winds, she helped two sailing dinghies which had been capsized in the strong winds during the afternoon, with the lifeboat spending an hour at sea helping the sailors who could not right their craft. On 25 May, in two separate incidents, she helped two motor vessels, one of which had broken down while the other had run out of fuel. Further services were completed in June and July, and on 11 August D-196 performed what proved to be her final service at the station. She launched in light northerly winds to a broken down motor boat and brought it to safety.

▼ A fine photograph of D-196 at sea on exercise. She served the station for fifteen years and saved forty-seven lives during that time. (Colin Watson)

1987 – 1996

The C class inflatables

In 1986 the station was upgraded to operate a twin-engined C class inflatable. The decision to station the larger C class inflatable at Red Bay had been made in 1984 after the Chairman of the station, T. G. McLaughlin, had written to Tony Course, the RNLI's Divisional Inspector, expressing the view that the single-engined D class ILB was not adequate for the coastal areas which the station covered. The letter was, in turn, passed to Commander Michael Woodroffe, Staff Officer Operations, and as a result the RNLI agreed to send a relief C Class inflatable, C-505, to undertake evaluation trials at Red Bay in spring 1985.

The service which prompted the letter from T. G. McLaughlin had been undertaken on 9 September 1984. D-196 was called out at 6.45am by the Coastguard to search for three men who left Cushendun in a 16ft rowing boat at 7.30pm the previous evening. They were recovered safely by helicopter at 8.30am on 9 September. However, during the search from Red Bay to Torr Head by the ILB, her crew had faced very challenging conditions, which, in the view of the Chairman, were hazardous to negotiate in a single-engined boat. Conditions at the launch site were good, but once the ILB was at sea and approaching Torr Head the sea became extremely rough. The crew had the drogue ready in case the engine failed, and the letter stated, 'if it had failed, I dread to think what the result would have been. This coast is very steep and barren. There are no other boats available, and both tide and currents are as bad as anything around the coast.'

The C class inflatable was the obvious step up. It was a 17ft 6in Zodiac Mk.II craft, powered by twin 40hp outboard engines, making it faster, with a top speed of approximately thirty knots, and more powerful than the D

▶ The relief C class inflatable C-505 is put through her paces during her nine-month stint at Red Bay. Built in 1978, she served at St Abbs for seven years before entering the Relief Fleet. After her time at Red Bay, she went to a new station at Clifden on the west coast of Ireland.

◀ Lifeboat crew and station personnel with the station's first C class inflatable C-505, which served from August 1986 to May 1987.

class. The type had been introduced to the RNLI fleet in the late 1970s to fit in between the larger Atlantic 21, which would later come to Red Bay, and the D class inflatable. Manned by a crew of three or four, it could be righted manually after a capsize, and employed a buoyancy system which was specially designed by the RNLI to allow the boat to continue on service even if the bow was punctured. Similar equipment to the standard D class inflatable was carried, but the C class also had a battery-powered spotlight for night-time operation.

The relief boat C-505 served at Red Bay from August 1986 to May 1987, during which time she undertook four services, including one on 8 November

1986 after a yacht got into difficulties half a mile east of the station. The two sailors on the yacht were unable to right their craft after it capsized in force seven winds, and so the ILB was launched to help. The lifeboat crew brought the yacht to safety, saving the two sailors, thus completing a service that would not have been undertaken in the D class which was only on operational duty until 31 October each year.

While the relief boat was serving Red Bay, a new Zodiac was built for the station, number C-519, which was placed on station on 25 May 1987. She was named Thomas Corbett and had been funded by the trustees of the Thomas Corbett Charity. The formal dedication of the new boat was held at Cushendall on 21 May 1988. The ceremony was chaired by the branch chairman, Mr T. G. McLaughlin, who thanked the community for its willing support of the lifeboat service. The ILB was accepted by Vice-Admiral Sir Arthur Hezlet, Vice President of the RNLI, on behalf of the Institution, and Neil Workman, honorary secretary, accepted the boat into the safekeeping of the station. The service of dedication was conducted by the Rev Francis Park, assisted by Canon Bannon, the Rev R. S. Ross and the Rev H. McEldowney.

The first service by C-519 Thomas Corbett was carried out on 8 July 1987 when a person fell from a cliff ten miles south east of the station, and the lifeboat was out for over two hours providing assistance. The other three services undertaken during 1987 were all to small boats. The following year, 1988, proved a busy one with no fewer than fifteen services completed, mostly routine in nature. On 16 May 1988 C-519 towed in a fishing boat, which had engine problems off Garron Point, and landed its two crew. Two

▼ The relief twin-engined C class inflatable C-505, which served from August 1986 to May 1987.

◀ The scene during the naming ceremony of the C class inflatable C-519 *Thomas Corbett*.

▼ After the naming ceremony, the C class inflatable C-515 is launched for a demonstration.

months later, on 17 July, C-519 was launched after a red flare was spotted two miles south of Glenarm Bay. The ILB was quickly on scene and found a 21ft fishing boat with a rope around its propeller. Together with its three crew, the boat was safely brought to Glenarm harbour by the ILB.

The summer of 1990 saw the Red Bay lifeboat volunteers in demand, with the first of several services during the season coming on 9 July to a fishing boat which had engine trouble off Garron Point. The ILB launched in force five winds and towed the boat back to Carnlough harbour. Five days later the lifeboat was in action again in strong winds, undertaking two services

1987 – 1996

▶ The lifeboat crew helped local residents during the flooding in Ballycastle and Cushendall in October 1990.

to yachts, one with a broken rudder and the second with a broken mast. On 2 August a 26ft yacht with five people on board broke its rudder and was towed to shore by the ILB. On 15 August a windsurfer, swept out to sea at Waterfoot beach, was saved by the ILB, and on 30 September a 16ft capsized sailing dinghy was brought to safety.

Memories of the C class

"When our C class Thomas Corbett (C-519) arrived, it seemed so much bigger and more capable than the D class boat. For a start we had the luxury of twin engines! With twin engines, if one went down you still had another to get out of trouble. With the single-engined D class, if the engine stopped you were in trouble. The manoeuvrability was fantastic with the boat turning on a sixpence, even at high speed, but the g-force generated in such a turn could throw a crewman out of the boat.

The twin engines also allowed the boat to turn in a circle, within its own axis, with one engine ahead and one astern. So although the boat was quite a bit bigger overall than the D class, it was actually a lot easier to work with close inshore around rocks. In high seas the C class stuck to the water like glue, due in part to the extra lead weight on the forward edge of the keel area. In fact, the bigger the sea conditions the more she liked it, providing a ride like a rollercoaster, and inspiring a feeling of safety and confidence among the bleak grey mountains of water, which was often all you could see.

If the wave pattern was a short, sharp chop, then the C class became a very different animal. That same lead weight turned against it and it would bump and bang over the short seas to the groans and grunts of the poor crew. It wasn't unknown for injuries to happen. Knee joints, wrists, even heads banged together, although the full face motorcycle helmets provided good protection.

There were very few C class boats in the RNLI fleet overall, and a lot of stations and crews will never even have seen one. So I think it is nice that Red Bay had one for so long, and that it played such a major part in the history of our station to date."

Gerry O'Neill

The most notable incident in which the Red Bay lifeboat crew were involved during the year, however, did not involve the lifeboat. In the early hours of 18 October 1990 the towns of Ballycastle and Cushendall were badly flooded, and the lifeboat crew were involved in the efforts to rescue people trapped by the flood waters. The river Tow had burst its banks at Ballycastle and a large number of people were stranded as a result. The crew assembled at 5.40am to be briefed by the Deputy Launching Authority about the extent of the flooding in Cushendall and Ballycastle. Two small 16ft fibre glass open boats were provided by Red Bay Boats Ltd, and the lifeboat crew teamed up with fire crews from the fire brigade to provide assistance. The rescue teams split into two groups, which immediately set about systematically searching the flooded areas in the mid Glens. Weather conditions were poor, the wind was easterly force six and it was raining throughout the operation.

The rescuers checked every property and car, struggling through water that was, in most places, waist deep, although in some areas it was deeper with 10ft of water along the riverside. At 6.30am one of the boats had to go a mile upriver to a family who had been completely cut off and were trapped inside their bungalow, with 4ft deep floodwater running fast through their kitchen. The family was taken out through a window and carried to high ground and safety. Meanwhile the main search party was still at Cushendall, searching each house and property. The rescue work continued throughout the day until about 4pm, with help given to many people cut off in their homes as well as to farmers whose livestock was stranded in the nearby

▼ C-519 Thomas Corbett leaving Cushendall on exercise. (Colin Watson)

fields. At 10.30am two crew and one of the 16ft boats were despatched by road to assist a farmer near Glenariff four miles away. The boat was launched into the floodwater to lift livestock, mainly sheep, to safety.

At 10.45am three other crew members, with a small inflatable, again went by road to help in the flood relief work at Ballycastle, where the flood waters had still not receded and the situation was still critical. They helped to bring six more people to safety in Ballycastle. Cushendall police requested further assistance in the Glenariff area at 1.45pm, where more livestock had become cut off by the flood waters. Five lifeboat crew members were despatched to the scene with one of the 16ft boats, and they helped to bring fourteen sheep to safety. By 4pm the flood waters had receded sufficiently for the authorities to declare the emergency over, with all inhabitants of the Cushendall area accounted for.

Following this service, framed letters of thanks were sent by the RNLI's Chairman to the station, stating: 'The whole operation proved to be a fine display of co-operation between the lifeboat crew members and the local fire brigade. Your tireless efforts were greatly appreciated by the local community and brought great credit to the lifeboat service'. The letters were received by Deputy Launching Authority D. McCollam and crew members Tom McLaughlin, Patrick McLaughlin, Donald McAlister, Liam McCollam, Joseph Ferris, Peter McLaughlin, Andrew McAlister, Niall McCambridge, Patrick McCambridge, James Farrell and Joe Burns for their services given to the civil authorities during the flood relief operations.

Further routine services were undertaken in 1991 and 1992. On 20 August 1991 the lifeboat launched to a cabin cruiser with a seized engine, and saved the cruiser's five occupants. The vessel was drifting when the alarm was sounded, but the lifeboat was quickly on scene to help the vessel and its crew. On 22 December 1991 a windsurfer was caught out by gale force winds

▼ C-519 towing in a broken down yacht.

▲ The twin-engined C class inflatable C-519 Thomas Corbett served Red Bay for eight years.

and was swept out to sea. He managed to fire a distress flare and C-519 was immediately launched to bring him to safety. On 12 April 1992 two fishermen were rescued after the propeller of their boat had become fouled by a loose rope. They managed to fire distress flares, despite the rough seas, and the lifeboat brought them to safety in Cushendall.

Between July and November 1992 the relief C class inflatable C-520, which had originally served at Criccieth, was on temporary duty at Red Bay while C-519 Thomas Corbett was taken to the RNLI's Inshore Lifeboat Centre at Cowes for survey and overhaul. During her four-month stint at the station, C-510 carried out four services, two of which resulted in assistance being provided to the casualties. On 27 July she went to a sailboarder who was in difficulties in force five winds, and brought him and his board to safety. On 13 August she went out to another sailing dinghy and saved five people who were on board. C-519 returned to station on 20 November 1992, and went out on 6 December to three sailing dinghies which had got into trouble in strong force six winds, bringing all three to safety.

In August 1993 C-519 and her crew were involved in a major search after two divers failed to surface near their support boat off Rathlin Island. The alarm was raised by the boat's crew after the two men, who had been exploring sunken wrecks off the Island, failed to come to the surface after being under water for thirty-five minutes. A full-scale land, air and sea search was launched after the distress call had been picked up by a Royal Naval patrol vessel. C-519 was quickly launched to help in the search, which also involved the Portrush lifeboat and a helicopter. However, the divers were spotted by the Naval patrol vessel and picked up safe and well, with the rescue units stood down.

1987 – 1996

On 2 May 1994 the relief C-512, originally stationed at Cullercoats, was involved in an unusual service when she went to help an injured crew member from the small tanker Northern Star, which was carrying chlorine from the south coast of England to Derry. The ILB launched at 6am to the tanker, which was eight miles south east of Torr Head. One of the tanker's officers had fallen ill and the doctor recommended he be taken off the ship immediately and transported to hospital. The lifeboat brought him ashore to a waiting ambulance at Cushendall and he was transported to Antrim Hospital, where he was treated for vomiting and diarrhoea before being discharged. Most medical evacuations such as this one are carried out by offshore lifeboats, and for the Red Bay ILB this was a very unusual incident. C-512 was on emergency relief duty at Red Bay from 22 April to 2 June 1994, and this was the only service she performed.

C-519 Thomas Corbett returned to station in June 1994 after emergency repairs, but only served at Red Bay for just over another year. On 28 July 1995 she left the station and was temporarily replaced by the relief C class inflatable C-523 British Diver IV, but in the event C-519 never returned and C-523 remained at Red Bay until 2 April 1996.

C-523 was involved in a very challenging search in 1995, during which she and her crew spent more than seven hours at sea. She launched at 2.50pm on 27 August 1995 to assist Portrush lifeboat Richard Evans (Civil Service No.39) in a search for a missing German diver in rough seas and swell up to seven metres in height. The initial search by C-519 was undertaken south of Rathlin Island, but after three hours, a crew change and refuelling took place at Ballycastle. The ILB rejoined the search at 7.15pm, this time gong to the north side of Rathlin Island together with the Portrush ALB, where the C class inflatable faced the full force of the north-westerly gale. After

▼ Launching the C class inflatable on exercise in 1988. This photo gives an idea of the effort involved to man handle the craft, on her trolley, into the water.

◀ Visit to Red Bay lifeboat station by HRH The Duke of Kent (second right) in 1996, with (from left to right) T. G. McLaughlin Snr, Honorary Secretary Neil Workman and Joseph Ferris with RNLI Director Brian Miles on right.

searching for a further hour and a half in the severe conditions, the search was called off and all units returned to station. While Portrush ALB was returning to station, the diver activated his emergency flashing light, which was seen by the crew, and he was successfully rescued. Following this service a letter of appreciation was received at the station from Commodore George Cooper, the RNLI's Chief of Operations, in which he said: 'I would like to add my own congratulations to those of the Portrush lifeboat crew, for the fine seamanship displayed by the Red Bay crew members who participated in this heavy weather service, which was marginal for a C class lifeboat.'

C-523 was involved in an unusual exercise on 1 October 1995, when she was tasked to search for four cases of oranges which had been purposely jettisoned from the Royal Navy minesweeper HMS Arun off Rathlin Island, together with group of divers. The object of the exercise was to discover

◀ Joseph Ferris served on the crew and was later Honorary Secretary.

The Glens Lifeboat Guild

For many years, the people of both Ireland and the UK have held the RNLI in their hearts. Towns and villages throughout the country have raised money for the charity, even though many have not had any direct connection with the sea. Almost every town has had its RNLI Branch dedicated to raising money for 'The Lifeboats'.

In the Glens of Antrim for as long as can be remembered the local communities have raised money for the charity. The closeness to the sea and the many people whose livelihood have depended on the sea, has meant that the RNLI has been close to their hearts. In the Glens collections have been made for the charity for as long as can be remembered. Call in to any shop in the area and you will find a lifeboat collection box prominently placed on the counter.

A short time after the formation of the lifeboat station at Red Bay, many local residents, wanting to assist, decided to form a Lifeboat Guild to support the activities of the crew. The Lifeboat Guild is a group formally setup as an association, recognised and affiliated to the RNLI, with the aim to organise the fundraising activities within their local area. The Glens Lifeboat Guild, established in 1985 by among others T. G. McLaughlan Snr (now President of the Guild), continues to be active in its fundraising role.

The Guild is made up of members of the community of all ages who come together to support a cause that they feel is a very important aspect of Glen's life. They meet regularly in the lifeboat station and are able to liaise with and meet other local branches, fostering their aim to raise funds, in a sociable and enjoyable way.

Each year the Guild, working in parallel with the crew and the staff of the lifeboat station, hold various fundraising events, from coffee mornings, cheese and wine parties, raffles, and the annual open day is held at the start of the Cushendall Festival week in August.

The Guild has been fortunate in having the support of local artist Sam McLarnon UWS. Since being approached by Liam McCollam, Sam has donated one of his original landscape paintings each year to Red Bay Guild. This has been used as the major prize in our annual draw, and in 2009 the draw raised over £1,000.

▼ The scene during lifeboat day in 2004 when hundreds of people visit the station and it is the main fund-raising day of the year.

where the oranges would go ashore and to monitor the drift of the long-suffering divers, so that the tidal streams in the area could be monitored more accurately. The scheme, which involved the Coastguard, Royal Engineer divers, HMS Arun, the Army Air Corps and the RAF in addition to the lifeboat was prompted by the incident in August 1995, when a German diver spent almost eight hours in the water, and a similar incident in which divers drifted for four hours before being picked up by a passing yacht. The complicated tidal currents and wind flows off Rathlin and in the approaches to the North Channel made it very difficult to calculate how far people and objects would drift, and during this exercise the divers were swept no less than fourteen miles from their predicted position in only four hours. During the exercise Red Bay lifeboat and Ballycastle coastguards were called to a real incident to recover a man from the bottom of a cliff.

On 23 January 1996 a service was undertaken which demonstrated the determination and commitment of the Red Bay crew. The incident started after the tug Point James lost power just off Torr Head, eight miles north of the station. The Coastguard requested a launch, so crew members Tom McLaughlin, Andrew McAlister, Paddy McCambridge and Liam McCollam prepared to put to sea. As the slipway was being repaired, the boat had to be taken to a slipway five minutes' drive away on her road trailer, but the weather was so bad that launching from there was not possible. As the situation with Point James was critical, a helicopter was tasked, but with the

▲ C-519 Thomas Corbett returning to station having taken a sick man off the small tanker Northern Star in May 1994, which was heading for Derry. The ILB was launched at 6am to the tanker and landed one of the ship's officers, who was taken to hospital by ambulance at Cushendall.

rain and low cloud it was not certain if the aircraft would be able to take the crew off the tug.

So the lifeboat crew decided to try and launch C-523 off a nearby beach, something they had never done before. The boat was towed down a narrow path, across a river and onto the shingle, then taken off the trailer and turned head to sea. The helm, Tom McLaughlin, climbed on board, while the rest of the crew held the bow to the sea. They were operating in force seven winds, at the limits of the ILB's capabilities, and it took ten minutes, with the crew up to their necks in the breaking seas, before they could get the boat away. One crew member stepped down due to exhaustion, and his place was taken by Larry McAfee. Once under way, C-519 headed for Torr Head, making slow progress in the conditions and by far the worst experienced by the crew. After fifteen minutes the boat had only travelled about two miles.

Meanwhile, Campbeltown lifeboat Walter and Margaret Couper had been launched to provide support and was making best speed in horrendous conditions across the channel from Kintyre. At this point, the Coastguard radioed to say that the helicopter was on scene and winching off the crew. They asked if the ILB still wanted to proceed to provide back-up for the helicopter, but the radio-operator, Andrew McAlister, did not even bother to consult his helm and bluntly stated 'we are heading home, unless it is really essential'. No one argued! The journey back to station was very difficult, with the boat close to capsizing a couple of times. Indeed, at times some of the crew could have been thrown out of the boat. The ILB had to be recovered

▼ Red Bay lifeboat crew with C-519 outside the lifeboat house.

◀ C class inflatable C-519 Thomas Corbett launching from the slipway at Cushendall.

at a local pier as a normal recovery was impossible, but the crew and boat made it home safely. While this callout, undertaken in darkness with strong winds, driving rain and heavy seas, may not have had a successful outcome in terms of assistance provided, it demonstrated the spirit and courage of the local crew and their commitment to life-saving. Out at sea, the crew of Point James were all successfully rescued by a skilful Royal Navy crew.

This service not only demonstrated the commitment of the Red Bay crew, but also showed that the demands made on them were sometimes difficult to be met by the C class inflatable. As this class of lifeboat was, by the mid-1990s, being phased out of service and replaced by the larger Atlantic rigid-inflatable at most stations where they had operated, the turn of Red Bay to get the bigger boat came in 1996. C-523 stayed at Red Bay until 5 April 1996, and then another relief C class ILB, C-514, was sent to the station so that C-523 could return to Cowes for emergency repairs. C-514 stayed until 12 June 1996, launching once on service, on 6 April, to save a man who had gone overboard from his motor boat. This proved to be the last service carried out by the C class ILBs at Red Bay and, as they departed, a new chapter in the station's history began.

▼ Neil Workman, who served as Honorary Secretary for twenty years, was awarded the MBE for services to the RNLI.

1996 – 2010

Upgrade to an Atlantic

By the time the first of the station's Atlantics, B-527 Percy Garon, was in service, a new lifeboat station was being constructed. The old boathouse was too small to house the new, larger lifeboat as well as its launching rig, so a completely new building was erected on the same site as the old house. The new boathouse provided considerably better facilities, with housing for the lifeboat and launching vehicle, a changing/drying room, workshop, fuel store, shower and toilets, a crew/training room, and a galley and store. At the same time, the slipway was widened to make launching and recovery of the lifeboat easier and safer.

The first Atlantic, B-527, had been built in 1974 and served at the busy Southend-on-Sea station in Essex for ten years before entering the Relief Fleet. Named Percy Garon, she had been funded by the Civil Service and Post Office Lifeboat Fund. As a relief lifeboat, she served a number of stations and arrived at Red Bay on 3 June 1996 after visiting Skerries, north of Dublin, and Clifden lifeboat stations for launching trials as both stations were also being upgraded to operate Atlantics. At Red Bay, she took over rescue duties on 12 June after extensive crew training had been completed and stayed until early September 1996, undertaking six launches during her short stint.

While the relief Atlantic 21 was on duty, the station's own new Atlantic 75 was under construction, being fitted out at the RNLI's Inshore Lifeboat Centre at Cowes. The new boat, B-728, was funded from the bequests of Miss Dorothy Mary Raine and Mr David Stanley Raine and was named Dorothy Mary. She arrived at Red Bay in late August 1996 and was placed on station on 3 September. The Atlantic 75 represented the RNLI's second

▶ In front of a crowd of supporters and well-wishers, B-728 Dorothy Mary is launched at the end of her naming ceremony for a demonstration run.

generation of rigid-inflatable B class inshore lifeboats, having been developed from the Atlantic 21 which was gradually replaced by the 75. One of the main improvements the Atlantic 75 had over the 21 was the ballast tank at the front of the boat, which enabled the boat to launch into heavier surf than the 21. The boat was powered by twin 75hp outboard engines and could reach speeds in excess of thirty knots.

The naming ceremony for the new lifeboat was held on 19 October 1996, when not only was the new lifeboat named Dorothy Mary, but the station's new boathouse was officially opened. Clayton Love Jnr, deputy chairman of the Institution, opened the boathouse and Paul Clark, an Ulster Television personality, named the lifeboat. RNLI Director, Lt Cdr Brian Miles CBE, represented the donors and handed the lifeboat into the care of station honorary secretary Neil Workman during the ceremony.

Although the new lifeboat was first called out on service on 14 October 1996, a few days before the inauguration ceremony, others coped with the capsized sailing dinghy to which she launched and she returned to station without being needed. Her first effective service came on 16 June 1997, when she towed the yacht Bluff to safety. A busy summer followed with several launches during the rest of June and in July and August, the lifeboat and her crew assisting a variety of craft including yachts, motor boats, dinghies and divers. A similar type and number of rescues were undertaken

Memories of the first Atlantic ILBs

"The 1990s saw the Red Bay Station continue to thrive with an enthustic team of volunteers from the local community. The building of the current station and upgrade to the Atlantic 75 brought renewed vigour to the station. While the new facilities and slipway were being built, we had to work out of temporary facilities for over a year and for launching we used another local slipway at Dalriada.

With the upgrade to the Atlantic 75, crew training moved up a gear with all crew attending intensive training courses at the RNLI training complex in the Isle of Wight. The week-long courses gave crew members the chance to meet lifeboat crews from other stations and learn superb skills in a different environment.

With the faster and larger Atlantic inshore lifeboat, the crew were able to reach causalities faster, and in some comfort! The weather conditions around the North Antrim coast can be very challenging and many times we worked in difficult conditions, especially round the coast of Rathlin along with our colleagues from Portrush.

The loss of several crew due to age presented the station with a number of challenges. In one twelve-month period five experienced crew members with years of experience had to retire. But, thankfully, the remaining crew and the introduction of a new generation of enthusiastic people enabled the station to go from strength to strength.

The strength in any lifeboat station is the people and the community in which they serve. Red Bay has had many great characters over the years, with everyone having different strengths, and when you fit these together it is amazing to see the results of people's efforts, sometimes in very difficult circumstances. We have had fun and many laughs and happy memories."

Paddy McLaughlin

in 1998, including two rescues in a day on 2 August 1998. The first service was to a 14ft pleasure craft with five persons on board, which was brought to Red Bay after the vessel suffered engine failure. The second was to a jet skier who fell off his craft near Waterfoot beach in the evening, and he was rescued by the lifeboat crew after a member of the public raised the alarm.

One of the most difficult incidents in which the Red Bay crew have been involved concerned two brothers who took their own lives, two weeks apart, in May and June 2000. The sequence of events began on 23 May when a man approached one of the crew, about the man's brother. He was worried because he was missing from the previous night and had been threatening to drive off a local pier. Tom contacted another crew member and they went down to the boathouse to meet the informant, unsure whether to take the man seriously but phoned the Honorary Secretary to ask if the lifeboat could be launched. The boat was launched and started to search, and soon a car was seen just off the pier in about 20ft of water. A local crew member who was also a diver volunteered to take a look, but as a person was still in the car a Police diving team was tasked to recover the body, being assisted by the lifeboat.

This, however, was not the end of the tragedy. Less than two weeks later another report was received of a car and person missing, off the same pier. The lifeboat again launched and the crew soon spotted a car in the water. Again one of the crew volunteered to dive down to the car, but on this occasion no person was found to be inside the car. So a widespread search began, involving the lifeboat, a helicopter, local coastguards and local boats, covering the whole area in driving rain and rough seas. Initially nothing was found, and the family who arrived to help search were in despair. They lived ten miles inland and were farmers, and the lifeboat house became their base as the crew helped search both land and sea. A bond was formed between the family and the local crew as the family members saw the crew as the only people who could help them find the body and end their despair. The searching continued for nearly two days before the police dive team were available to help. The lifeboat again assisted with a final sweep before calling off the search, at which point the body was found and brought back in the boat to the boathouse. One of the most poignant aspects of these incidents was the fact that both the deceased had taken their lives in the same way. They both drove off the same pier at a similar time, both in the same make and colour of car.

Unfortunately the search for and recovery of bodies is part of the work of lifeboat crews. While the primary aim is always to try to save life at sea, when this is not possible it is important to give families closure by returning the bodies of their loved ones. There have been many times when the lifeboat has returned with a body on board, either as a result of an accident or because they took their own lives. This can be very traumatic for the crew and the strong bond between the crew and station personnel becomes

▲ The impressive lifeboat house for Atlantic 75 and launching tractor completed in 1996. (Nicholas Leach)

◀ The second lifeboat house at Cushendall is demolished to make way for the new building.

particularly important for providing mutual support at difficult moments.

A successful search was undertaken on 19 August 2001 after the motor boat Canute, on a fishing trip from Carnlough Harbour with four persons on board, got lost in the fog. With visibility less than fifty metres, and the boat's GPS equipment proving faulty, the four crew contacted Belfast Coastguard to say they were lost. B-728 Dorothy Mary was launched with Tom McLaughlin on the helm and Paddy McLaughlin, Ruairi McNaughton and Jimmy Healey making up the crew. As the ILB was not fitted with VHF D/F or radar equipment, the crew had to go on the last known accurate GPS position of the casualty. The lifeboat began a expanding box search and the crew also made radio contact with Canute requesting that they blow a whistle to make finding them easier. Larne all-weather lifeboat was also tasked but, after thirty-five minutes, on one leg of an expanding search box, the ILB came across Canute, some of whose crew were not wearing appropriate foul-weather clothing and at least one of whom was shivering from the cold. With Larne lifeboat closing quickly, it was decided to rendezvous with the ALB and transfer the potentially hypothermic casualties to that, after which the ALB escorted the casualty south to Carnlough. B-728 proceeded back to station, arriving at about 5.25pm.

▼ Red Bay lifeboat crew and station personnel with Atlantic 75 B-728 Dorothy Mary. (Colin Watson)

1996 – 2010

◀ B-728 Dorothy Mary emerging from the lifeboat house on her do-do carriage. (Nicholas Leach)

◀ Launch on exercise of B-728 Dorothy Mary in June 2000. (Nicholas Leach)

▼ B-728 Dorothy Mary putting out on exercise. (Nicholas Leach)

▲ B-728 Dorothy Mary launching from Cushendall through an onshore swell in 1998. (Supplied by Red Bay RNLI)

On 15 April 2002 B-728 Dorothy Mary was launched to the 30ft cabin cruiser Victory, which was on passage from Coleraine to Belfast when its engine failed a mile and a half north of Cushendun. The vessel had been blown towards rocks and was in imminent danger in very rough seas when the lifeboat arrived on scene. Once close to the casualty, the lifeboat crew rigged a tow and in a three-hour operation successfully towed the craft to Cushendall. A Royal Naval patrol boat was also tasked to help with the rescue operation and stood by to assist if required. After the rescue, helmsman Paddy McLaughlin commented, 'conditions were very poor with a two-metre swell and strong winds. It was quite a difficult operation. The man was very glad to see the lifeboat crew arriving.'

Just over four months later, on 24 August 2002, the lifeboat crew were involved in an incident on what seemed to be a particularly pleasant afternoon, with a cloudless sky, and a gentle offshore breeze which had tempted most of the local dinghy sailors onto the water. At 3.43pm B-728 Dorothy Mary was called out after one of the sailing dinghies, with three men on board, got into difficulty. The men had set out for a sail around the bay, with one wearing a wetsuit and the others in shorts and tee-shirts. All three were wearing lifejackets, but the boat had neither oars nor an engine.

In the sunshine and gentle conditions they attempted to sail a little further up the coast, but a combination of factors resulted in the situation getting out of control. The three men had little experience and no local knowledge so they were oblivious to the fact that the tide had turned and was sweeping them towards one of the roughest areas on the north coast. They struggled in vain for two hours to sail back towards Red Bay, but found themselves swept into the overfalls at Torr Head, an area where tides can reach eight knots. The dinghy soon became swamped and could not sail fast enough for the self bailers to work, leaving the men terrified, sitting waist deep in a cockpit full of water and two without wetsuits starting to suffer from hypothermia. To make matters worse, the boat's owner, the most experienced of the three, had received a heavy blow to the head from the boom. Although awash, the dinghy's built-in buoyancy kept it afloat.

Fortunately the skipper of a 42ft motor boat on passage to Ballycastle spotted the dinghy in the heavy seas off Torr Head and, having managed to get the men aboard, reported to Belfast coastguard. At this point the Atlantic 75 was launched, heading at full speed towards the area, which was reached in fifteen minutes. The men were more than happy to remain in the safety and comfort of the larger yacht for the duration of the passage to Ballycastle, where an ambulance would be waiting to check their medical condition. The crew of the lifeboat offered to tow the swamped dinghy to Murlough Bay, but this proved an arduous task. The return passage to station was somewhat slower as the tide was against the lifeboat, which diverted to deal with another incident, a small fishing vessel with engine trouble. The lifeboat returned to station at 7.10pm and was ready for service half an hour later.

▼ Atlantic 75 B-728 Dorothy Mary at speed off Cushendall while on exercise. (Nicholas Leach)

▲ In strong winds B-728 Dorothy Mary rescues the crew from a fishing vessel which had broken her moorings and was being swept out to sea in force ten winds, October 1997. The crew on board the lifeboat were Sinead McCollom, Dave Bowen and Gerry O'Neill.

On 8 September 2002 the Red Bay lifeboat and her crew were involved in a very testing rescue. The yacht Chloe, on passage from Gigha Island to Carnlough, was being sailed in rough seas by an elderly couple. Although they were in no immediate danger, negotiating the entrance to Carnlough Harbour in the prevailing wind and sea conditions would be difficult, while the yacht's inboard diesel engine would not start, meaning that entering the harbour would be impossible in the conditions. The skipper of Chloe explained his predicament via radio to Belfast Coastguard, who in turn discussed the matter with the Honorary Secretary. It was decided launching the Atlantic would be prudent and B-728 put out at 12.10pm manned by Tom McLaughlin, Paddy McLaughlin, James Healy and Gareth Shannon to rendezvous with Chloe and provide whatever assistance was necessary. An extra crew member, with considerable sailing experience, was taken as it felt his experience would be invaluable.

The ILB reached Chloe fifteen minutes after launching, but, in the force six winds, gusting to force seven and very rough seas, was unable to go alongside the pitching and yawing vessel. The tidal rips off Garron Point produced large breaking seas and the transfer of an ILB crew member onto the casualty vessel was not possible until both vessels reached a calmer area. At an opportune moment, Gareth Shannon was transferred across to the casualty and took over the helm. This gave some respite to the elderly couple and allowed one of them to go below to rest, while Chloe continued to Carnlough. The other remained in the cockpit, where she felt reassured by the presence of the lifeboat crew.

Chloe made slow but steady headway under sail toward Carnlough, where on arrival it was apparent that the sea conditions were worse than expected and manoeuvring the heavy vessel safely through the entrance of Carnlough Harbour would be challenging. Local Coastguard personnel on shore were

◀ Station personnel, RNLI officials and crew members outside the lifeboat house. From left to right: Sean McAuley, Larry McAfee, Andrew McAlister, two RNLI committee members, Charles Stewart, Sir Jock Slater (RNLI Chairman), Neil Workman, Padraig Mitchell, Colin Williams (RNLI Inspector), Gerry O'Neill and Paddy McLaughlin.

able to inform the ILB crew of the sea conditions at the entrance to the harbour, and helm Tom McLaughlin decided that it was a better option to make for Glenarm marina. Chloe was too heavy for the ILB to tow, and the sea state was too great for the Atlantic to manoeuvre the stricken yacht through the tight marina entrance . The swell had increased with breaking waves at the entrance to the marina so the helmsman requested the help of the Larne all-weather lifeboat.

Larne lifeboat Dr John McSparran, under the command of Coxswain Frank Healy, met the Atlantic 75 and the casualty vessel about a mile north of Glenarm and crew member Paul Johnston was successfully transferred onto the Atlantic 75 and then onto the yacht to attach a secure towing line to the bow. The Atlantic 75 passed a restraining/controlling line to the stern of the casualty and together the lifeboats carefully and deliberately manoeuvred through the entrance of the marina, negotiating a difficult turn in the process. A crowd of onlookers watched the manoeuvre as Chloe was berthed over two and a half hours after the Red Bay lifeboat had launched. The lifeboat crews had worked as a team, and the help given to the elderly couple was greatly appreciated. Although the shore crew at Red Bay had prepared the trailer for a net recovery, by the time the ILB had returned conditions had settled and the lifeboat was recovered in the normal fashion.

Following this service, helmsman

▼ B-728 Dorothy Mary and her crew on service off Garron Point on 24 June 2001 when three people were saved from the small dory, which sunk, throwing its occupants into the water. The crew are, from front to back, Gary Fyfe, Emmet Connon and Larry McAfee.

The Dorinish Buoy

Any visitor to Red Bay lifeboat station cannot fail to miss the Dorinish Buoy, located beside the car park close to the station. The Buoy was acquired from the Commissioner of Irish Lights (CIL), the organisation that maintains the lighthouses and navigation buoys around Ireland. Joseph Ferris, Lifeboat Operations Manager (LOM) at the time, managed to obtain the structure and arranged for its installation by the station so that it could act as a collection box for the RNLI

The buoy, conical buoy No 131, was built in 1969 and spent most of its life moored in Clew Bay, Co Mayo, opposite Inishgort lighthouse. It warned mariners to keep clear of the shingle bar at the northern end of Dorinish More. Replaced by a younger and more modern buoy at this location, the old buoy spent a few years out of the water at the Ferris Point Depot, Islandmagee, near Larne. It had become a bit of a rusty hulk with no lantern or radar reflectors although the steelwork remained in perfect condition.

After an agreement had been reached with the CIL that the buoy could be brought to Red Bay, the lifeboat crew transported it from Larne, with the Larne lifeboat used to tow the buoy north. Once at Red Bay, the buoy was shot blasted and cleaned, a collection slot was made in the side and a plaque was attached to commemorate the buoy. The original green paint work was replaced by lifeboat colours with lettering and logos to match. A solid foundation and finish was prepared and the buoy was lifted into place. The lantern works and the collection box has its steady trickle of generous patrons.

Soon after the buoy had been installed, the CIL vessel Granuaile paid a visit and Captain George Ball, First Officer Desmond O'Brien and a shore party arrived in Red Bay for a formal handing over ceremony of the new buoy, with lifeboat crew, committee members, councillors, and a piper in attendance.

◀ The Dorinish Buoy, an old navigation marker operated by the Commissioners of Irish Lights, outside the lifeboat house.

1996 – 2010

◀ Presentation of Thanks Inscribed on Vellum to Tom McLaughlin by Colin Williams (RNLI Divisional Inspector) in Belfast in May 2003 for the service in September 2002 to Chloe. The crew pictured with Colin Williams (on left) are, from left to right, Tom McLaughlin, Jimmy Healy, Paddy McLaughlin, and Gareth Shannon.

Tom McLaughlin was accorded the Thanks of the Institution on Vellum, while crew members Paddy McLaughlin, Jimmy Healy and Gareth Shannon received letters of appreciation. The actions of Larne lifeboat were also recognised by a joint letter of appreciation. Deputy Divisional Inspector, Owen Medland, praised the teamwork of both crews for the successful outcome of the service, saying: 'A plethora of lifeboating skills were demonstrated by all on board'. Owen singled out Tom's actions, which prevented the rescue escalating into a more serious situation, adding 'Tom McLaughlin showed great foresight and command during the service'.

On 1 August 2004 B-728 Dorothy Mary assisted two casualties in one service in an incident that started after a fisherman at Torr Head observed a small craft with two persons on board experiencing difficulty in the

▼ Relief Atlantic 75 B-724 Rotarian Dennis Cullen on exercise with Larne lifeboat, 44ft Waveney The William and Jane.

◀ Honorary Secretary Joseph Ferris firing a maroon to mark the end of their usage, watched by, left to right, Andrew McAlister, Jimmy Healy and Gerry O'Neill.

strong overfalls off the headland. While on passage to the casualty crossing Cushendun Bay, the ILB crew became aware of a slow speedboat moving erratically off Tornamona Point. A small course change took the ILB alongside the second vessel without losing much time and the lifeboat crew found that the two persons on board were suffering seasickness and the boat's steering was broken. As the vessel was making way, albeit slowly, and the two persons were in no imminent danger, the helmsman decided to proceed to the original casualty. This was reached quite quickly and the ILB crew found another vessel, the charter RIB Predator, alongside the casualty offering reassurance. The ILB helmsman and charter skipper agreed it was best that the two casualties on the vessel be transferred to the charter boat and a tow should be set to the charter boat to take them home. The ILB assisted with this operation, which was made difficult by the strong tidal overfalls.

Once the two persons were safe and the tow set, the ILB returned to the broken down speedboat and took the two persons on board. By this stage one of them was extremely seasick and the crew decided it sensible to administer oxygen to help. The ILB then set a tow to the speedboat and made for Cushendun. The seasick casualty was monitored carefully and given oxygen underway to Cushendun. In time he started to feel better and the helmsman decided there was no need to summon further medical assistance. Coastguard personnel were waiting in Cushendun as the ILB arrived and the two persons were transferred into their care. The ILB then returned to Predator and while, the two persons stayed aboard Predator which quickly returned to Red Bay, the ILB towed the casualty vessel back.

On 25 July 2009 B-728 Dorothy Mary was involved in a ten-hour rescue operation to free a man trapped under rocks at Fair Head. The lifeboat launched at 2.30pm and did not return to the station until after midnight. As well as the Red Bay lifeboat, the operation involved the Irish Coast Guard helicopter, the Coastguard cliff rescue team and members of the specialist fire and rescue unit from Belfast all working together to free the casualty, who was in a dangerous and difficult to reach location on the cliff face.

▲ B-728 Dorothy Mary on exercise with Portrush lifeboat William Gordon Burr in December 2009 during a major search and rescue exercise off the Antrim coast.

▲ B-728 Dorothy Mary on exercise with Portrush lifeboat in December 2009. For the exercise, the lifeboats were joined by the Irish Coast Guard helicopter from Sligo and the Ballycastle Coastguard, and the exercise was carried out in the Ballycastle Bay and Rathlin Sound area, with Charles Stewart (above) at the helm of B-728.

▶ Neil Workman on board B-728 Dorothy Mary, with the crew in background, to mark his MBE award.

Once on scene, two lifeboat crew climbed the rocks to administer oxygen to the trapped man, who was pinned under rocks and specialist equipment was needed to free him. The Irish Coast Guard helicopter brought members of a specialist fire and rescue unit from Belfast including a doctor, and because of the remote location lifting the rock and hoisting the stretcher with the seriously injured man up to the helicopter was a major operation. The location was so remote that the rescue team had to undertake a dangerous walk to the base of the cliffs and return by Red Bay lifeboat to land.

Helmsman Paddy McLaughlin said afterwards: 'It was a very difficult rescue operation. The location of the incident meant that everyone had to work together as radio communication was poor and the terrain was very dangerous. We were all conscious of the urgency of the situation and our focus was to get the casualty and the rescue personnel out of there safely and quickly. Conditions early on were calm but as the night progressed they worsened significantly.' The man was taken to the Royal Victoria hospital in Belfast, where he later recovered from his ordeal.

▶ B-728 Dorothy Mary leaving Ballycastle harbour after an exercise with Portrush lifeboat and the search and rescue helicopter in 2009.

▲ Having been re-fitted with an orange sponson, B-728 Dorothy Mary launches on exercise in July 2010, a few months before she left Red Bay. She served the station for almost fourteen years and saved more than 200 lives in that time. (Nicholas Leach)

2010 –

The Atlantic 85

▶ On board B-843 Geoffrey Charles on the station's open day in 2010. On board are, from left to right, John Walsh, Kevin Allen, Donal McAlister and Paddy McLaughlin.

In July 2010 a new Atlantic 85 lifeboat arrived at Red Bay and, after a period of intensive crew training, was placed on station on 29 July. The new boat, number B-843, replaced B-728 Dorothy Mary, which had served the station for almost fourteen years, during which time she was launched 187 times and rescued 227 people. One of the 75's last callouts involved working alongside the Portrush lifeboat William Gordon Burr on 8 June 2010 to rescue six people from the Ocean Youth Trust vessel Lord Rank, which grounded and sank off Kinbane Head while on passage from Ballycastle to Portrush. The vessel was engaged in a charity fund-raising event and was scheduled to call at a number of Northern Ireland ports. She had completed her fund-raising activities at Ballycastle and left there at 9pm with three crew and three passengers on board. On clearing the breakwater at Ballycastle, the vessel headed in a northerly direction. About

▶ Atlantic 85 on exercise shortly after she had first arrived on station.

ten minutes later the vessel altered course and ended up going aground on Carrickmannanon Rock at about 9.23pm, resulting in the service by the two lifeboats to rescue the people on board.

The Atlantic 85 was the latest development of the RNLI's B class rigid-inflatable inshore lifeboat. Fitted with radar interfaced with GPS and VHF direction-finding equipment, it was powered by two 115hp outboard engines giving a top speed of thirty-five knots. Other improvements on its predecessor include provision for a fourth crew member and more space

▼ Atlantic 85 B-843 Geoffrey Charles being launched from the do-do trolley. (Nicholas Leach)

▲ B-843 Geoffrey Charles on exercise with Larne lifeboat Dr John McSparran in June 2010, the day the Atlantic 85 was placed on service.

for survivors. It can operate safely in daylight in conditions up to force seven and at night in up to force six, and is also capable of being beached in an emergency. The boathouse doors of the station had to be widened to accommodate the new boat, which was launched from a larger carriage.

The new £165,000 lifeboat, funded by a gift of Mr and Mrs Colmer, was named Geoffrey Charles after the donors' son, and brought a new dimension to life-saving off the Antrim coast. Speaking on the arrival of the new Atlantic 85, a crew spokesman said, 'We are delighted with our new lifeboat. The improvements mean a faster response time and more space for taking on board casualties. We have huge support here from the community and from visitors to the area. I hope this new lifeboat has many successful years ahead of it.' Within the first few months of the new boat's arrival, the crew undertook intensive training, including exercises with the rescue helicopter based at Prestwick and the neighbouring lifeboats from the Portrush and Larne stations.

The first service performed by the new Atlantic 85 was undertaken during the evening of 7 August 2010. The lifeboat launched to help two people, a brother aged twenty-three and his sister, aged fourteen, who had got into difficulty in the Boulder Field on Fair Head rocks. The call was received at

▼ Atlantic 85 B-843 exercising with Rescue 177 helicopter in June 2010.

2010 –

◀ Atlantic 85 B-843 Geoffrey Charles putting out on exercise (Nicholas Leach)

6.25pm when the siblings went walking in the Boulder Field and got into difficulty. The lifeboat was launched and was soon on scene, with the crew having to deal with a heavy swell as they manoeuvred their boat close to the rocks. One of the lifeboat crew swam from the lifeboat onto the rocks with another crew member's drysuit and a lifejacket, and assisted the casualties one at a time using a rope. Under difficult conditions, the two casualties were recovered onto the lifeboat and landed at Ballycastle. Commenting on the rescue afterwards, helmsman Paddy McLaughlin said, 'Although people like to walk in this scenic area of North Antrim it can be a very dangerous spot. This was a successful first callout for our new lifeboat and the two people are recovering well from their ordeal.'

▼ Atlantic 85 B-843 Geoffrey Charles off Cushendall. (Nicholas Leach)

2010 –

▶ Portrush lifeboat William Gordon Burr, seen from the Atlantic 85 B-843, saving two people from a small pleasure boat, 16 May 2010. B-843 towed the boat to Ballycastle while Portrush lifeboat landed the two survivors at Ballycastle, where an ambulance took them to hospital.

During the afternoon of 18 September 2010 the new lifeboat was again in action, rescuing three fishermen off Cushendall. The three men were in a 14ft boat when the weather deteriorated severely, with gale force eight winds catching out the men. They managed to make their way to nearby cages kept in the sea by a salmon farm and raised the alarm. In the gale force winds and rough seas, B-843 was launched and the lifeboat crew rescued the men from the cages in a fairly straightforward operation, despite the difficult conditions. They were taken safely back to shore, and the lifeboat towed their vessel to safety. The men, who had borrowed the boat from a friend and were at sea for the first time, were very cold and wet, but uninjured. The rescue operation was coordinated by Belfast Coastguard, who had some difficulty as the casualties spoke little English.

▼ B-843 Geoffrey Charles returning to station form exercise. (Nicholas Leach)

2010 –

▲ B-843 on service in October 2010 to a broken down motor boat, which had been tied to fish farm cages by its three crew.

◀ B-843 Geoffrey Charles on exercise in March 2011. (Nicholas Leach)

▼ Red Bay lifeboat crew and station personnel 2011 with B-843.

▲ B-843 Geoffrey and Charles heading back to station with the Antrim coast forming the backdrop. (Nicholas Leach)

On 13 November 2010 the lifeboat crew put their first aid training into practice after a man collapsed while out walking in Boulder Field at Fair Head. The lifeboat was launched at 3.55pm to the incident and on arrival at the scene the lifeboat crew were able to locate the two men among the rocks. Two lifeboat volunteers left the lifeboat with first aid equipment to give assistance to the casualty. However, to reach the men they had to climb 150ft up the rocky terrain carrying their equipment. The Royal Navy helicopter Rescue 177 from Prestwick arrived a short time later with a paramedic and was able to stabilise the casualty and winch both him and the other man aboard, before taking them both to Coleraine Hospital. Commenting on the callout, a lifeboat spokesman said, 'Thankfully we are very familiar with this area and two of our lifeboat crew were able to use their first aid training and go to the assistance of the casualty. This is not an easy area to access and the two men had been out walking since breakfast.'

Lifeboat summary

On station	Official Number	Name Donor	Dimensions Type
5.1972–1986	D-196	– –	15’6” x 6’3” RFD PB16
11.8.1986-21.5.1987	C-505	– –	17’6” Zodiac Mk.IV
25.6.1987–31.7.1995	C-519	**Thomas Corbett** –	17’6” Zodiac Mk.IV
28.7.1995–5.7.1996	C-523	– –	17’6” Zodiac Mk.IV
2.4.1996-12.6.1996	C-514	– –	17’6” Zodiac Mk.IV
3.6.1996–3.9.1996	B-527	**Percy Garon** Civil Service and Post Office Lifeboat Fund.	22’9” x 7’6” Atlantic 21
3.9.1996–7.2010	B-728	**Dorothy Mary** Bequests of Dorothy Mary Raine and David Raine.	24’ x 8’8” Atlantic 75
29.7.2010–	B-843	**Geoffrey Charles** Gift of Mr and Mrs Colmer.	8.3m x 2.8m Atlantic 85

Relief inshore lifeboats

1984 • D-185 • 5 June to 30 September
1987 • D-178 • 1 April to 26 June
1989 • C-520 • 18 August to 23 February 1990
1991 • C-523 • 26 April to 24 May
1992 • C-510 • 24 July to 20 November
1994 • C-512 • 22 April to 2 June
1997 • B-724 • 21 October to 30 April 1998
2000 • B-767 • 4 October to 20 July 2001

Relief D class inflatable D-185, built in 1970, served at Red Bay in 1984.

Service summary

D-196 inshore lifeboat

1972	Sep 14	Motor boat, saved boat and 4
	Oct 15	Motor boat, saved boat and 2
1973	Sep 1	Capsized yacht, saved yacht and 2
	2	Capsized yacht, saved yacht and 2
1975	June 13	Fishing boat in tow of motor launch Dublin, escorted boat
1976	May 27	Speedboat Helga, gave help
	June 12	Sailing dinghy Flying Dutchman, saved dinghy and 3
	July 4	Dinghy, gave help
	23	Rowing boat, gave help
	Aug 28	Dinghy, saved dinghy and 1
1977	June 20	Fishing boat RED BAY, gave help
	29	Motor launch, gave help
	July 3	Sailing dinghy, gave help
	23	Motor boat in tow of boat, escorted
	Aug 7	boat, gave help
1978	May 24	Motor boat, gave help
	July 15	Dinghy, gave help
	Aug 8	Dinghy, saved boat and 2
1979	May 6	Motor cruiser Anchor Plus, gave help
1980	May 14	Cabin cruiser, gave help
	Aug 19	Fishing vessel Red Bay, gave help
1981	Apr 19	Rubber dinghy, gave help
	June 29	Dinghy, saved boat and 4
	Aug 14	Motor cruiser, gave help
	22	Motor boat, gave help
	30	Motor boat, landed 3
1982	Aug 1	Motor boat, saved boat and 8
1983	Apr 6	Dinghy, gave help
	June 12	Sailboard, saved board and 1
	20	Motor boat, gave help
	July 19	Dinghy, gave help
	24	Motor cruiser, gave help

D-185 inshore lifeboat

1984	June 27	Sailing Club rescue boat, gave help
	July 8	Motor boat, gave help
	18	Cabin cruiser Corran, gave help
	25	Dinghy, gave help
	Aug 4	Sailing dinghy, saved dinghy and 2
	Sep 2	Dinghy, gave help

D-196 inshore lifeboat

1985	May 25	Sailing dinghy, saved dinghy and 2
	June 17	Cabin cruiser in tow of coastguard boat, escorted
	28	Catamaran Dobbin, saved boat
		Cabin cruiser Maggie Jane, gave help

C-510 inshore lifeboat

	July 11	Canoe, gave help
	14	Motor boat, gave help

D-196 inshore lifeboat

	20	Sailing dinghy, saved dinghy and 2
		Motor boat Dick Darby, saved boat and 5
	24	Motor boat Dick Darby, gave help
1986	Apr 6	Sailing dinghy, gave help
		Sailing dinghy, saved dinghy and 1
	May 25	Rubber dinghy, gave help
		Motor boat, gave help
	June 21	Cabin cruiser Carrick Diver, saved boat and landed 6
	22	Cabin cruiser Carrick Diver, gave help
		Motor boat, gave help
	July 21	Cabin cruiser Blue Horizon, gave help
	Aug 11	Cabin cruiser Blue Horizon, gave help

C-505 inshore lifeboat

	Nov 18	Two persons overboard from sailing dinghy, saved dinghy and 2

D-178 inshore lifeboat

1987	Apr 5	Yacht, saved craft and 4

C-519 Thomas Corbett inshore lifeboat

	July 8	Persons fallen from cliff, gave help
	Aug 15	Rubber dinghy, craft brought in– gave help
		Yacht, craft brought in– gave help
	25	Motor boat, craft brought in– gave help
1988	Feb 22	Cabin cruiser, craft brought in– gave help
	May 16	Motor boat, saved boat and 2
	July 17	Fishing boat, craft brought in– gave help
	29	Rubber dinghy, saved craft
	30	Motor boat, escorted boat
	Aug 6	Fishing boat, craft brought in– gave help
	14	Motor boat, craft brought in– gave help
	Sep 4	Fishing vessel, escorted
1989	Apr 2	Swimmer, landed a body
	July 2	Motor boat, craft brought in
	13	Power boat, craft brought in
	22	Motor boat, craft brought in
	26	Motor boat, craft brought in
	Aug 12	Persons cut off by tide, saved 1
1990	Mar 18	Sailboard, saved board and 1
	July 9	Fishing boat, craft brought in
	14	Yacht, craft brought in
		Yacht, craft brought in
	Aug 2	Yacht, five persons and craft brought in
	15	Sailboard, saved board and 1
	Sep 30	Sailing dinghy, saved craft and 2
	Oct 20	Unidentified canisters, gave help
1991	Jan 20	Sailboard, saved board

C-523 British Diver IV Relief ILB

May 5 Motor boat, craft brought in

C-519 Thomas Corbett inshore lifeboat

Aug 20 Motor boat, saved boat and 5
Sep 22 Sailboard, escorted
Oct 26 Motor boat, craft brought in
Dec 22 Sailboard, saved board and 1
1992 Jan 19 Sailboard, craft brought in
Feb 2 Motor boat, craft brought in
Apr 12 Power boat, craft brought in
May 23 Power boat, craft brought in
June 14 Motor boat, craft brought in
21 Motor boat, craft brought in

C-510 Relief inshore lifeboat

July 27 Sailboard, saved board and 1
Aug 13 Dinghy, saved dinghy and 5

C-519 Thomas Corbett inshore lifeboat

Dec 6 Sailing dinghy, gave help
Sailing dinghy, craft brought in
Sailing dinghy, saved dinghy and 2
1993 Jan 27 Motor boat, escorted
Apr 18 Fishing vessel craft brought in
July 25 Sailboard, craft brought in
Motor boat, craft brought in
Aug 3 Power boat, craft brought in
12 Motor boat, craft brought in
Oct 18 Power boat, gave help
1994 Jan 4 Fishing vessel Flora, stood by vessel

C-512 Relief inshore lifeboat

May 2 Sick man on board liquefied gas tanker Northern Star, sick man brought in

C-519 Thomas Corbett inshore lifeboat

Aug 21 Yacht Loose Lady, four persons and craft brought in
Sep 8 Fishing boat Homeward Bound, saved boat and 1
Oct 23 Sailing dinghy, saved boat and 1
Sailing dinghy, one person and craft brought in
Dec 29 Rubber dinghy, escorted boat
1995 Apr 16 Sailboard, saved board and 1
June 20 Cabin cruiser Claire, 8 persons and craft brought in
July 13 Yacht Darthvla, gave help

C-523 British Diver IV Relief ILB

Aug 15 Motor boat Steady Aim, landed 6 and craft brought in
20 Motor boat, saved boat
28 Tender to yacht, two persons and craft brought in
Sep 10 Person fallen from cliffs at Carrick-a-Rede, gave help
Speedboat, two persons and craft brought in
1996 Jan 15 Fishing vessel Crystelle, gave help

C-514 Relief inshore lifeboat

Apr 6 Man overboard from motor boat, saved boat and 1

B-527 Percy Garon Relief inshore lifeboat

Aug 1 Sheep, saved sheep
11 Fishing vessel Roisin Dew, landed 3 and craft brought in
11 Motor boat, four persons and craft brought in
19 Dinghy Ardnamurchan, escorted

B-728 Dorothy Mary inshore lifeboat

1997 June 16 Yacht Bluff, three persons and craft brought in
18 Diver support craft, saved craft and 1
22 Motor boat, saved craft and 3
July 6 Dinghy, saved dinghy and 2
14 Dinghy, two persons & craft brought in
16 Motor boat April, landed 1 and craft brought in
26 Yacht Oread, three persons and craft brought in
Aug 16 Two divers, landed 2
23 Motor boat, two persons and craft brought in
24 Yacht Svala, three persons and craft brought in

B-728 Dorothy Mary inshore lifeboat

1998 Apr 14 Motor boat Sea Hog, landed 4 and craft brought in

B-728 Rotarian Dennis Cullen Relief ILB

29 Dinghy, two persons & craft brought in
May 3 Man fallen from cliffs, gave help
Inflatable dinghy, three persons and craft brought in
17 Inflatable dinghy, four persons and craft brought in
June 26 Motor boat Sandrita, one person and craft brought in
July 14 Yacht Ballero II, in tow of craft Highland Laddy, escorted craft
24 Man fallen from cliff, gave help
25 Cabin cruiser, gave help
27 Cabin cruiser, saved craft and 6
Aug 2 Man overboard from jet ski, saved jet ski and 1
Speedboat, five persons and craft brought in

Service summary (continued)

	23	Motor boat Fairhead, two persons and craft brought in
	30	Cabin cruiser, landed 5 and brought in
1999	Apr 5	Angling boat, saved craft
	28	Man in sea, landed medics and an injured man
	July 10	Fishing vessel Red Bay, escorted craft
		Speedboat, landed 3 & craft brought in
	14	Inflatable dinghy Orra, landed 3 and craft brought in
	16	Motor boat, saved craft and 1
	30	Cabin cruiser Jeanie Ann, one person brought in and saved craft
	Aug 15	Sailing dinghy Laser Buzz, two persons and craft brought in
	21	Large power boat Megan, three persons and craft brought in
	Sep 2	Four people stranded, gave help
	5	Inflatable dinghy, landed 2 and craft brought in
2000	May 23	Car in the sea, landed a body
	28	Sailboard, escorted craft
	July 2	Man overboard from jet ski, landed 1, jet ski brought in and saved 1
	14	Motor boat Scots Wha Hey, two persons and craft brought in
	Sep 3	Powerboat, saved craft and 4

B-767 Maritime Motion Relief ILB

	Nov 22	Fishing vessel Investor M, assisted to save craft and 4
2001	Apr 14	Yacht Sabre, saved craft
	21	Powerboat Lorenzo, one person brought in
	22	Cow, gave help
	June 23	Man overboard from yacht, craft brought in
	24	Cabin cruiser Saturn, landed 2 and craft brought in
		Six people stranded, gave help
	25	Powerboat, four persons and craft brought in
		Angling vessel Lady Linda, landed 5 and craft brought in

B-728 Dorothy Mary inshore lifeboat

	29	Cabin cruiser, three persons and craft brought in
	July 28	Powerboat, two persons and craft brought in
	Aug 19	Powerboat Canute, escorted craft
	Sep 9	Speedboat, landed 4 & craft brought in
	Nov 2	Cabin cruiser Midnight Star, two persons and craft brought in
	4	Cabin cruiser Sea Breeze, landed 6 and craft brought in
2002	Mar 3	Cabin cruiser Iona, landed 3 and craft brought in
	Apr 4	Fire on cliff path, gave help
	15	Cabin cruiser Victory, saved craft and 1
	May 5	Powerboat, landed 3 and saved craft
	6	Powerboat, gave help
	23	Person stranded, saved 1
		Fish farm workboat, saved craft and 1
	June 1	Powerboat, three persons and craft brought in
	6	Dive support craft, three persons and craft brought in
	17	Jet ski, landed 2 and craft brought in
	July 20	Rowing boat, landed 1 and craft brought in
	21	Powerboat Seashell, four persons and craft brought in
		Cabin cruiser, saved craft and 4
	Aug 21	Jet ski, one person & craft brought in
	24	Sailing dinghy, craft brought in
		Yacht, landed 1 and craft brought in
	28	Speedboat, two persons and craft brought in
	Sep 1	Speedboat, two persons and craft brought in
	8	Yacht Chloe, gave help
	Oct 12	Rigid-inflatable boat Oban Tiler, landed 3 and craft brought in
	Nov 24	Sailing dinghies, stood by
	Dec 7	Yacht Carnelion, landed 2 and craft brought in
2003	Feb 11	Fishing vessel David Andrew, one person and craft brought in
	Mar 16	Yacht Xelor, one person and craft brought in
	May 24	Missing diver, gave help
	July 4	Yacht Rudha na Gael and tender, gave help
	28	Yacht Quandry of Antrim, four persons and craft brought in
	30	Yacht Sirona, seven persons and craft brought in
	Aug 3	Sailing dinghy Deja Vu, escorted craft
	29	People stranded on cliff, stood by
2004	Mar 14	Yacht Moyle Maiden, landed 6 and craft brought in
	Apr 4	Jet ski, landed 1 and jet ski brought in
	May 2	Injured child, three people brought in
	23	Angling vessel Boy Conal, escorted
	July 25	Angling vessel Renegade, two persons and craft brought in
	28	Human body, landed a body
	Aug 1	Powered boat, craft brought in
		Powered boat, two persons and craft brought in

28 Child at risk, landed 1
31 Swimmers, two people brought in
2005 June 25 Powered boat Cuchulainn, one person and craft brought in
July 14 Yacht Honora, gave help
15 Powered boat, landed 2 and craft brought in
17 Powered boat, two persons and craft brought in

B-792 Joseph and Mary Hiley Relief ILB

22 Powered boat, two persons and craft brought in
Aug 13 People stranded on rocks, landed 2
16 People missing, gave help
Sep 17 Powered boat Misty Flare, one person and craft brought in
Oct 24 Person at risk, landed a body

B-728 Dorothy Mary inshore lifeboat

2006 June 20 Yacht Cushag of Mann, four persons and craft brought in
Aug 1 Powered boat, landed 2, craft brought in and saved 1
Sep 5 Powered boat, two persons and craft brought in
2007 June 5 Yacht, four persons and craft brought in
9 Canoes, two craft brought in
People cut off by the tide, one person brought in
July 12 People cut off by the tide, landed 1 and one person brought in
Aug 20 Powered boat, three persons and craft brought in
Sep 16 Jet ski, landed 1 and jet ski brought in
Oct 11 Canoe, craft brought in and saved 1
2008 Mar 19 Fishing vessel, craft brought in
May 10 Powered boat Jamjack, two persons and craft brought in
June 9 Inflatable dinghy, craft brought in
Powered boat Yellow Glen, one person and craft brought in
July 3 Yacht Suki of Shuna, two persons and craft brought in
23 Tender, craft brought in
Powered boat Myna, escorted craft
26 Powered boat, landed 5 and craft brought in
Aug 10 Inflatable dinghy, craft brought in
14 Yacht Mentor, five persons and craft brought in
24 Yacht White Hawk, landed 2 and craft brought in
Oct 12 Powered boat Clonara, two persons and craft brought in
2009 Jan 2 Powered boat Boisterous, assisted to save craft
12 Tractor, gave help – illuminated scene
Feb 21 Powered boat Nicole, two persons and craft brought in
Mar 1 Tender, craft brought in

B-754 Pride of Sherwood Relief ILB

May 26 Yacht Razor Edge, escorted craft
28 Powered boat, two persons and craft brought in
June 13 Injured man on cliff, landed 1
July 20 Powered boat Merry Fisher, two persons and craft brought in
25 Powered boat, two persons and craft brought in
Climbers, one person brought in and assisted to save 1
Aug 6 Powered boat Wendy Lou, two persons and craft brought in
16 Powered boat Still Deep 1, escorted
20 Powered boat Artis Thern, one person brought in

B-728 Dorothy Mary inshore lifeboat

Oct 1 Powered boat Ruthless Hunter, craft brought in and saved 2
2010 Mar 2 Dog, gave help - rescued dog
Apr 10 Powered boat, six people and craft brought in
May 16 Powered boat Tight Lines, saved craft
26 Powered boat, three people and craft brought in
June 8 Sail training vessel Lord Rank, gave help – transferred casualty to Portrush ALB
26 Yacht Hanna Rose, four people and craft brought in
27 Powered boat My Little Traz, three people and craft brought in
Powered boat, two people and craft brought in

B-843 Geoffrey Charles inshore lifeboat

Aug 7 People cut off by tide, saved 2
Sep 2 Powered boat, gave help
18 Powered boat Red Devil, craft brought in and saved 3
19 Yacht Makatea, two people and craft brought in
Oct 13 Powered boat two people and craft brought in
17 Sailing dinghies, landed 3
Nov 13 People stranded at Fair Head, gave help – administered first aid
Dec 10 Powered boat Jaggy Rose, gave help – illuminated scene

Station personnel and crew

This book is dedicated to all the volunteer crew and station personnel who have served on the lifeboats at Red Bay and are listed here.

Joseph Ferris
Liam McCollam
Donal McAlister
Alan Murphy
Tom McLaughlin
Andrew McAlister
Paddy McLaughlin
Peter McLaughlin
Patrick McCambridge
Gerry O'Neill
Alister Rowan
Dan McCollam
Gary Fyfe
Aidan O'Neill
Ruairi McNaughton
Gerry Shannon
Peter McKillop
William Carey
Jimmy Healy
Francis Healy
Cormac Corish
Emmet Connon
Sean McAuley

Gareth Shannon
Michael Elliott
Joe McCollam
Claire Fyfe
Charles Stewart
Patrick O'Hagan
Garry McAlister
Kevin McGill
Kevin Allen
Donnell Black
Stephen Conway
Padraig Mitchell
Emmet McManus
Neal Blaney
Paul McAlister
Kevin McDonnell
Derry Shannon
Dr Louise McIlwaine
Kerri O'Neill
John Walsh
John Aicken
Kevin McAuley
Sean McAuley

Bobby McMullan
Donal McAlister Jnr
Sean Harvey
Matthew Bowen
Rita O'Neill
Samuel Goligher
Darren McGinley
James Sharpe
Dr Jimmy Clearkin
Michael McLaughlin
John McLaughlin
Dr A. J. McSparran
Tom Naughton
Tim Boyle
Neil Workman
T. G. McLaughlin
David Bowen
Larry McAfee
Sinead McCollam
Joe Burns
Michael O Hara
Dominic Miskelly
Peter Clerkin

John Blaney
Michael Jones
Chris O Neill
Niall MCCambridge
Chris McCarthy
Oliver McCollam
Robert McCollam
Terence McCollam
Joan Murphy
Norris Murray
Oliver McMullan
Hugh Ward
David Murphy
Patrick McCollam
Con Emerson
Robert Gilliland
Charles Metson
James Farrell
Alex McMullan
John McMullan
Joe McCollam
Hugo McCollam
Dr Dermot Grant

This book is also dedicated to all of the people who have helped fundraise and supported the station in any way.

Honorary Secretaries

Thomas Scollay	3.1972–11.73
Joseph Mitchell	11.1973–12.76
Mannix McAlister	1.1.1980–12.80
Neil Ross Workman	1.1.1981–6.2002
Joseph Ferris	21.6.2002–12.06
Alan Murphy	12.2006–

▶ Alan Murphy was appointed Lifeboat Operations Manager (title previously known as Honorary Secretary) in 2006, having previously been on the crew since the 1970s.